animals**animals**

Beavers

by **Wil Mara**

 **Marshall Cavendish**
Benchmark
New York

Marshall Cavendish Benchmark
99 White Plains Road
Tarrytown, New York 10591-9001
www.marshallcavendish.us

All Web sites were available and accurate when this book was sent to press.

Library of Congress Cataloging-in-Publication Data

Mara, Wil.
Beavers / by Wil Mara.
p. cm. — (Animals animals)
Summary: "Describes the physical characteristics, habitat, behavior, diet, life cycle, and conservation status of the beaver"—Provided by publisher.
Includes bibliographical references and index.
ISBN-13: 978-0-7614-2524-3
1. Beavers—Juvenile literature. I. Title. II. Series.

QL737.R632M23 2007
599.37—dc22

2006019710

Photo research by Candlepants Inc.

Cover photo: Clive Druett, Papilio/Corbis

The photographs in this book are used by permission and through the courtesy of:
Getty Images: Jeff Foott, 1. *Corbis:* W. Perry Conway, 4; Tom Bean, 16; Niall Benvie, 26; Robert Holmes, 30; Lynda Richardson, 34; Larry Lee Photography, 36; Hulton-Deutsch Collection, 37; Paul Souders, 39; Kent News & Picture/Sygma, 40. *Photo Researchers Inc.:* Barbara Stmadova, 6; James Steinberg, 14. *Peter Arnold Inc.:* Patrick Frischknecht, 11; Lynda Richardson, 21, 25; pa1240623, 31. *Minden Pictures:* Michael Quinton, 12, 22; Jim Brandenburg, 17, 38; Roel Hoeve/Foto Natura, 27; Konrad Wothe, 32; Rinie Van Meurs/Foto Natura, 42. *Super Stock:* Ingram Publishing, 24. *Art Resource, NY:* Smithsonian American Art Museum, Washington, D.C., (detail) 28.

Printed in Malaysia
6 5 4 3 2

Contents

1 Introducing the Beaver

Perhaps you have heard the phrase "as busy as a beaver." It refers to the fact that beavers are among the busiest creatures on earth. They seem to spend little time at play. Instead they work almost from the moment they wake until they go back to sleep. They are among the great builders of the animal kingdom, creating homes for themselves called *lodges*. Like little engineers, they also build *dams* that control the flow of streams and rivers. To do all this building, they use trees. They cut them down with their large and powerful front teeth.

Beavers are often found living and working in family groups. They tend to stay together, avoiding

Beavers are great builders. They use trees to make their homes and to control the flow of streams and rivers.

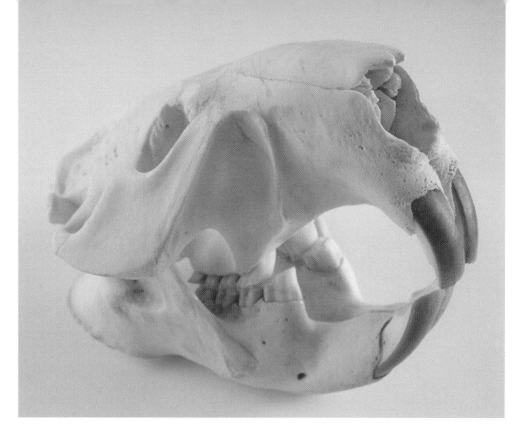

One of the major differences between the European beaver and the American beaver is the shape of the bones around the nose. Other than that, there is little that sets them apart.

people and most other animals. Humans in particular have hunted beavers for thousands of years, almost driving them to *extinction.* But beavers have survived, and they continue their wondrous ways.

There are two *species*—or kinds—of beavers in the world. One is known as the American beaver. The other is called the European beaver (or the Eurasian beaver). The two species look much the same. The only major difference is in the shape of the skull bones around their noses. Some experts also believe the European beaver does not spend as much time building as the American beaver. Female European beavers may also have their babies when they are older, and have slightly smaller *litters* than their American relatives.

Beavers are found in both the Old World (the Eastern Hemisphere) and the New World (the Western Hemisphere). The European beaver lives in parts of Europe and Asia, including France, Poland, Germany, Russia, Sweden, Norway, and Finland. The American beaver lives across North America, except in the extreme cold of northern Canada, the deserts of the United States, and most of Florida.

A beaver is brown and furry, with a long body, webbed hind feet, and tiny eyes. It is also known for its thin front paws that look similar to human hands, four large teeth in the front (two on top, two on bottom), and its scaly tail that is shaped like a paddle. A beaver is a nervous creature that can seriously injure a human if it is chased or cornered. If you ever see one, do not try to approach or touch it.

A beaver's teeth are one of its most important parts. Beavers cut down trees by chewing through them at the base of the trunk. The four large teeth in the front are called *incisors.* They are curved inward

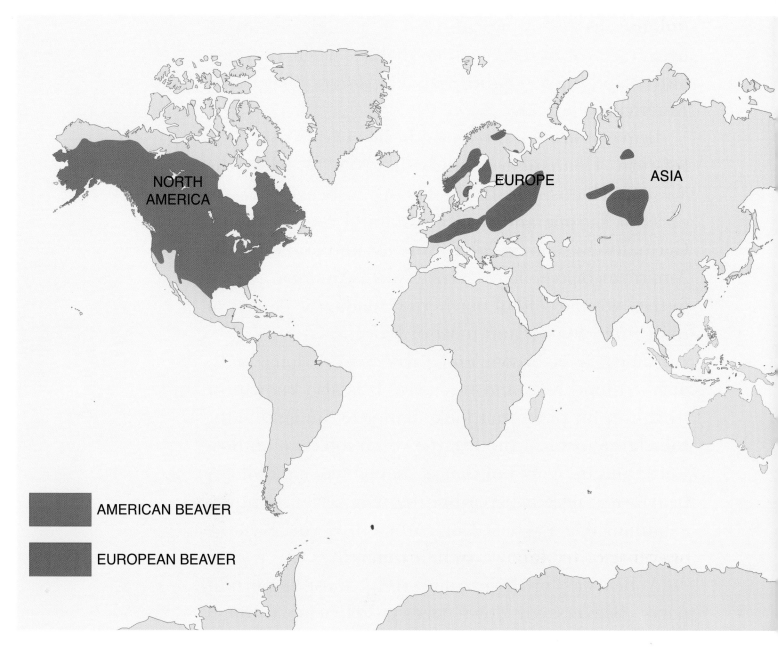

NORTH
AMERICA

EUROPE

ASIA

AMERICAN BEAVER

EUROPEAN BEAVER

Beavers are found throughout North America. They also live in parts of
Europe and Asia, but they are not as common there.

and have a yellowish orange coating. Beavers also have sixteen smaller teeth in the back of their mouths. These are used to grind up food.

Two flaps of skin in a beaver's mouth play a special role. They come together to form a large "plug" behind the incisors. It ensures that a beaver will not swallow any splinters or wood chips while it is gnawing a tree or chewing on an underwater branch.

A beaver's tail is long and oval shaped. It is dark brown to black, and it has a scaly texture similar to the body of a snake. The beaver uses its tail to steer when it is swimming. The tail also helps a beaver keep its balance while standing on its hind legs. A third and important way beavers use their tail is to "talk" to one another. When a beaver is alarmed, it will slap its tail on the water's surface. This serves as a warning signal to other beavers that danger is near.

A beaver has large glands near its tail that make an oil called *castoreum*. It is a syrupy liquid that a beaver uses to waterproof its furry coat. Beavers also use some to mark their territory, usually by putting it on a mound of mud. When other beavers notice the

Species Chart

Length (body): 28 to 36 inches (71 to 91 centimeters)

Length (tail): 9 to 17 inches (23 to 43 centimeters)

Weight: 30 to 60 pounds (13.5 to 27 kilograms)

Height (ground to shoulder): 10 to 14 inches (25.5 to 35.5 centimeters)

Coloration: Medium brown with reddish tones on top, light brown with ashy gray underneath. Older beavers often have streaks of white or light gray.

Life Span: Ten to fifteen years

A North American beaver floats a freshly cut branch across a pond.

Did You Know . . .

A beaver's front teeth never stop growing. If a beaver did not do so much chewing, its teeth would grow so long the beaver might not be able to open its mouth to eat.

A beaver's tail has many uses. It helps with balance and with steering when the beaver swims. It also serves as a warning signal. This beaver slaps the water to send the message that danger is near.

12

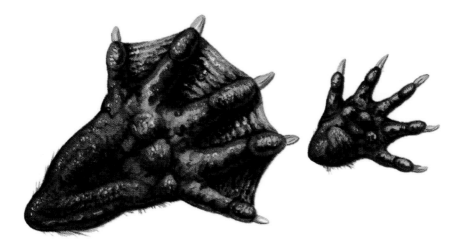

A beaver's front feet (right) are similar to a human hand, with long "fingers" used for grasping and pulling. The hind feet (left) have webbing, which helps a beaver swim.

scent of this oil, they know the area has already been claimed.

A beaver's front legs are short, and each foot has five long and powerful claws. The beaver uses the claws to comb and clean its fur. The back feet are webbed, making them perfect for swimming.

2 How Beavers Live

Beavers are *nocturnal* animals. Part of the reason they are active mostly at night is that many of the animals that hunt beavers are active during the day. These animals include wolves, bears, coyotes, otters, and people.

Beavers spend a great amount of time working on their lodges. They build their houses right in the water, whether it be moving (like in a stream or river) or still (as in a lake or pond). Sometimes they even "create" a pond or small lake first by building a dam. A dam is a wall that blocks the flow of a moving body of water. It causes water to back up and slow down almost until it stops flowing. The beavers begin a

A typical beaver lodge. You could easily mistake it for a pile of sticks and mud. Instead, it is home to a group of beavers.

*Beavers prefer trees
that are not too wide.
They are easier to chew
into smaller pieces.*

dam with mud, stones, and brush, creating a base under the water. Then they pile up more brush and mud, plus larger sticks, logs, and poles. Beavers continue working on a dam for weeks, months, and even years, adding to it or fixing it as needed.

Sometimes a beaver dam causes flooding in the nearby area. This can result in damage to homes and other buildings. In other places, normal or light amounts of flooding can help restore and improve the health of wetland communities that have dried out. Plants and animals that are drawn to wetlands can thrive once again.

When the beavers have found or created a body of water large enough to work with, they begin building their lodge. A lodge looks like little more than a messy pile of sticks and branches. It is often caked with mud for added strength. There is a large main room inside (sometimes more than one) where the beavers live. The floor is a few inches above the water level. It is often covered with grass, leaves, and wood chips.

Beavers are always working to improve their lodges and dams. If one springs a leak, the beavers waste no time in adding new wood to prevent their home from being flooded.

The Beaver:

A beaver has four large front teeth, long front claws . . .

Inside and Out

. . . and thick fur. It also has small eyes, common to animals that are active at night.

There is also a small hole in the roof to allow stale air to drift out. Beavers enter the lodge through underwater passages. Because of these special entrances, *predators* that target beavers cannot get inside the lodge. Most predators never realize this hidden opening is even there.

A family of beavers will remain in one lodge as long as there are enough trees nearby to eat and build with. Beavers prefer trees that are about 4 to 8 inches (10 to 20 centimeters) thick. To claim the tree, beavers stand at its base on their hind legs, turn their heads sideways, and begin chewing. They gnaw into one spot for a few moments, then move to the other side of the tree and begin work on another area. Over time they chew away enough of the base to cause the tree to fall. Usually they are able to get out of the way, but every now and then, a beaver is hurt or killed by a falling tree.

Once a tree is on the ground, a beaver chews off the leaves, branches, and bark. The main part of the tree is then cut into smaller pieces. The beaver brings each one back to the lodge. It rolls, pushes, or drags the logs. If this

Beavers don't use trees just for building—they also use them for food. They eat the leaves, smaller branches, and bark.

doesn't work, the beaver digs a trench from the forest to the water, waits for the trench to flood, then floats the logs back home.

Beavers use trees not only for building, but also for food. Once a tree falls, the beavers eat the leaves, branches, and bark. They eat parts of brushy shrubs, too, including the roots. They also like many aquatic plants, especially water lilies.

3 A Beaver's Life Cycle

A female beaver is able to give birth in her second year. Beavers mate in the winter in colder areas, and in the late fall where it is warmer. The babies develop inside the mother for a little more than three months—usually around a hundred days. This is called a *gestation period*.

The mother gives birth in late spring or early summer. The babies are called *kits* (and sometimes pups) and are usually born in groups—called litters—of two to four. The kits are already covered in fur and usually have their eyes open. If not, the eyes open in a matter of hours. Their coat—or *pelt*—is a slightly

A mother beaver has to make sure she has plenty of food in order to give birth to healthy babies. Having kits takes a heavy toll on the mother's body.

Beavers take excellent care of their young. They feed them, keep them warm, and protect them from predators for the first few years of their lives.

different color from that of their parents. It is often a reddish brown or a dark brown that appears almost black. A kit weighs anywhere from 9 to 20 ounces (0.25 to 0.56 kilograms) and measures about 12 to 16 inches (31 to 41 centimeters).

The mother nurses the kits for the first few weeks, often placing them on the underside of her tail so they can easily drink her rich milk. The babies are able to swim within just a few days. By the end of their first month, they start to explore outside the lodge. Their inner coat of fur is able to trap so much air at this stage that they often float on the water. Their oil glands also begin working after the first few weeks, protecting their fur from the cold water. Although their famous front teeth are not yet as strong or as large as their parents', they are still very sharp.

Beavers are natural swimmers. They are able to go into the water only a few days after they are born. The parents, of course, keep a close watch on their young anyway.

Young beavers stay with their parents for two to three years. After the first year, the parents have another litter. Mother beavers only have one litter each year. The young from the previous year help care for their newborn brothers and sisters. But once another year passes, the older beavers are "kicked out of the house" by their parents—mainly because there isn't enough room left in the lodge.

Young beavers grow fairly quickly and can have babies of their own within two years. By that time, the parents have cast them out of the lodge to make room for a new litter.

26

Beavers often stay together, as a couple, for a long time. They will have many litters over the years, two to four kits at a time.

The young beavers then go off in search of a home of their own. They rarely go far. Some die during their first year or two on their own, because they are not used to caring for themselves. Those that survive build their own lodges and dams, find their own mates, and have babies of their own. The normal life span of a beaver is between ten and fifteen years. Beavers sometimes stay with a mate for life. If one dies, however, the other will find a new mate. It is rare to see a fully grown beaver living alone.

4 Survival in the Wild

Beavers have a few main predators. They include wolves, wolverines, lynxes, and bears. Sadly, though, humans have become their greatest threat of all.

As early as the 1500s, and probably well before, people began trapping beavers. Beaver fur was prized because it is strong, warm, and *durable*. It holds together, lasts a long time, and is able to shed or resist water. The fur was used mostly to make coats and hats. It was perfect for people living in cold places. Beaver fur was also attached to the collars of coats made from other material, such as cowhide. Beaver pelts were eventually shipped around the world. They

For centuries, people used beaver fur to make clothing or to trade for other goods. Here, traders offer goods to Native Americans in exchange for their valuable beaver pelts.

Beaver pelts have been used to make everything from blankets and coats to fine felt hats. The fur keeps the head or body warm and dry, because it is thick and resists water.

were also traded for other items, such as food, guns and ammunition, and tobacco. Beaver fur became so popular that millions of beavers were killed. The European beaver did not avoid being hunted any more than its American cousin. Soon both species were almost extinct.

Beavers tend to avoid humans and most other animals that wander into their territory. The wolf is probably the beaver's main predator. Wolves are highly skilled hunters, and they will eat every part of a beaver. A single beaver can provide a wolf with a hearty meal.

Beavers are cautious of humans and predators. If a beaver senses any possible danger, it will dive into the water and disappear into its lodge.

A beaver's best escape route is underwater, where it can hold its breath for up to fifteen minutes if it has to.

Fortunately, beavers have become good at sensing when wolves are nearby. Experts have discovered that a beaver that picks up the scent of a predator will stay close to its lodge, even if it is hungry or eager to build. When a

32

predator manages to catch a beaver, it is usually because the beaver has strayed too far from its home. Beavers are especially at risk when searching for new territory. Young beavers are the easiest for predators to catch, especially those that have recently left the safety of their parents' lodge.

When a beaver senses danger nearby, it scurries back to the water and dives in. Even though beavers have lungs (like us) rather than gills (like fish), they can stay underwater for up to fifteen minutes. Normally, however, they stay underwater only three to six minutes. They tuck their small front legs against their bodies and kick their webbed hind feet as fast as possible. Their paddle-shaped tails steer them as they go. Beavers can swim about 1/2 mile (0.8 kilometers) before stopping to rest.

5 The Future of the Beaver

Beavers and humans have not always had the best relations. Some people tend to think of beavers as destructive or harmful creatures. Their actions can cause damage to homes, farms, roads, and other areas. Beavers need to constantly cut down new trees to build their lodges and dams.

Humans also use wood to build homes, furniture, and countless other items. When we cut down a forest in order to harvest the wood, we sometimes destroy the types of trees that beavers use and need most. When the trees are removed, the beavers that live nearby lose their source of food and building material. Also, as people build larger towns and cities,

A man offers a leafy treat to a beaver. Humans and beavers rarely come in such close contact. If you ever see a beaver, do not try and feed it.

Beaver dams often cause major flooding. While this is good for beavers trying to build lodges, it sometimes damages the places where people live or work.

more pollution is often created. Pollution has taken a huge toll on beaver populations, especially the chemicals that have spilled into waterways.

Beavers have come close to extinction. There was a time when there were millions of beavers in New York State. Through the years, that number dropped to hundreds of thousands, then to just a few thou-

This Nartive American felt a strong bond with beavers. It is not a good idea to lure beavers with food, though.

sand, a few hundred, then less than a hundred. Finally, the government stepped in to try and save them. In the late 1800s, laws were created protecting beavers from being killed in the wild. Government officials also had some beavers moved to places where former *colonies* had disappeared, in the hope of creating new ones. The plan worked, and soon there were hundreds of thousands of beavers again.

Beavers need plenty of trees in order to survive. The marks at the base of the trunk tell you a beaver lives nearby.

Conservation groups have made great efforts to save beaver populations. They have moved beavers to areas far from human communities. This has had mixed results.

This beaver is being released back into the wild. Beavers do not always survive the change. They can also bring disease to local animal populations.

Today there are few laws that protect either of the two beaver species. Some states have adopted rules that limit the number of beaver pelts a trapper can claim each year. But many others have not. While people still seek out beavers for their fur, it is much less common today than it used to be. Beavers are thus making a strong comeback. One reason is that they multiply fairly quickly. A healthy female can produce up to thirty or forty kits in her lifetime. Also, the wolf, which is one of the beaver's main predators, is becoming rare in certain areas.

Some *conservation* groups try to stop beavers from being destructive without harming the animals themselves. One method is to catch the beavers in a certain area and move them far from where people live. Since beavers tend to adjust easily to life in a new habitat (provided other beavers aren't already living there), this practice has turned out to be one positive course of action. As long as beavers have a large body of water and plenty of trees for eating and building, they are able to thrive. Unfortunately, moving beavers is not always a perfect solution. They can be exposed to diseases in a new place—illnesses they have never faced before. Some beaver populations that have been

Did You Know . . .
Beavers cause more than twenty million dollars in damage to homes, forests, and farmland every year.

moved to new regions have been wiped out by disease. Also, beavers can bring germs and viruses of their own into an area and harm the populations of other animals.

Meanwhile, people keep building. The more that human communities spread, the more space is needed. The earth has only so much room, and everyone needs enough space to live and grow. By working together and learning to share, we can ensure there will always be enough room for beavers in the natural world.

Glossary

castoreum—Oil produced by large glands near a beaver's tail, used by the beaver to mark its territory and to keep its fur waterproofed.

colony—A group of animals of the same species that lives together. With beavers, a colony usually consists of the two parents, the kits born most recently, and the kits born the year before.

conservation—The practice of keeping animals and environments safe from harm or destruction.

dam—A barrier or "wall" made by beavers from sticks, stones, mud, and other natural materials to control the flow of water in a river, stream, or similar body of water.

durable—Long lasting.

extinct—No longer existing; to have died out.

gestation period—The amount of time it takes for a baby (or babies) to fully develop inside a mother.

incisors—The four large teeth at the front of a beaver's mouth.

kit—A name for a baby beaver. It is also called a *pup*.

litter—A group of baby animals born to the same mother.

lodge—A beaver's home, built mostly from sticks, branches, logs, and mud.

nocturnal—Active at night rather than during the day.

pelt—The furred skin of a mammal.

predator—An animal that hunts and kills other animals for food.

species—A group of animals that has the same physical traits and that can mate and produce similar offspring.

Find Out More

Books

Becker, John E. *The North American Beaver.* San Diego, CA: KidHaven Press, 2002.

Frisch, Aaron. *Beavers.* Mankato, MN: Smart Apple Media, 2004.

Jacobs, Lee. *Beaver.* San Diego, CA: Blackbirch Press, 2003.

Long, Kim. *Beavers: A Wildlife Handbook.* Boulder, CO: Johnson Books, 2000.

Rue, Leonard Lee, III. *Beavers.* Stillwater, MN: Voyageur Press, 2002.

Web Sites

Animal Diversity Web pages for each beaver species
http://animaldiversity.ummz.umich.edu/site/accounts/
    information/Castor_canadensis.html

http://animaldiversity.ummz.umich.edu/site/accounts/
    information/Castor_fiber.html

Beavers
http://www.beavers-beavers.com/

Beavers: Wetlands and Wildlife Home Page
http://www.beaversww.org/

Enchanted Learning's Beaver Page
http://www.enchantedlearning.com/subjects/
    mammals/beaver.shtml

Wikipedia's Beaver Page
http://en.wikipedia.org/wiki/beaver

Index

Page numbers for illustrations are in **boldface**.

About the Author

Wil Mara has written many educational books for young readers, covering topics such as science, geography, sports, famous people, and other animals. Further information about these titles can be found at his Web site—www.wilmara.com